APOSTLES OF THE CITY

HOW TO MOBILIZE TERRITORIAL APOSTLES FOR CITY TRANSFORMATION

APOSTLES OF THE CITY

HOW TO MOBILIZE
TERRITORIAL APOSTLES
FOR CITY TRANSFORMATION

C. PETER WAGNER

Wagner Publications

Apostles of the City
Copyright © 2000
by C. Peter Wagner
ISBN 1-58502-006-0

Published by
Wagner Publications
11005 N. Highway 83, Suite 119
Colorado Springs, CO 80921
Email: wagnerpublicatons@globalharvest.org

Cover design by
Erin Mathis
emdesign Studio
1035 Tehama Avenue
Menlo Park, CA 94025
www.emdesignstudio.com

Interior design by
Rebecca Sytsema

Rights for publishing this book in other languages are contracted by Gospel Literature International (GLINT). GLINT also provides technical help for the adaptation, translation, and publishing of Bible study resources and books in scores of languages worldwide. For further information, contact GLINT, P.O. Box 4060, Ontario, CA 91761-1003, USA. You may also send e-mail to glintint@aol.com, or visit their web site at www.glint.org.

1 2 3 4 5 6 7 8 9   06 05 04 03 02 01 00

TABLE OF CONTENTS

CHAPTER ONE

OUR FRUSTRATIONS

Let me begin this book with two questions about city transformation that will help bring to light some extremely important issues which the expanding literature on how to reach our cities for Christ has not addressed in depth.

Question No. 1: Why is it that, in ten years of sincere efforts, we do not yet have one city in our nation with functional, ongoing, mutually-recognized leadership for effectively implementing a proven city transformation process?

Question No. 2: Why is it that, in city after city where an initial corporate vision for city transformation and a process for implementing it is in place to one extent or another, the Christian leadership commonly recognized as the most creative leadership in the city, has not actively participated in the design and does not actively participate in the practical fulfillment of the vision?

A Decade of
City Transformation Attempts

The reason I say "in ten years" is that the decade of the 1990s was characterized by, among other things, a strong consciousness among Christian leaders of all kinds that it is the will of God not only to save individuals and to gather them together in churches, but also to penetrate the entire society with the values and blessings of the kingdom of God. The unit of society most accessible to church leaders, the majority of whom are pastors, is the city in which they are currently ministering. Consequently, the idea of a city being changed caught fire across the country during the decade, and it arose in some other countries as well. It has been referred to in sermons and articles and books and classes as "city taking," "city reaching," "shaking a city," "revival in the city," "city transformation," and other terms.

George Otis, Jr., has spent several years identifying cities around the world in advanced stages of city transformation and documenting what has been happening in those cities. Of

---

◆

**A church
without active apostles and prophets
is a church
with an incomplete foundation.**

◆

---

the initial eighteen, only one of the cities clearly qualifies for the label in the past tense, "transformed." That is Almolonga, Guatemala. Twenty-five years ago a city of decadence, violence, drunkenness, disease, crime, poverty, idolatry, addiction, and misery; today it is a healthy, flourishing, happy, prosperous city with some 90 percent of the citizens born again Christians. The last jail was closed several years ago because there are no more criminals!

I mention Almolonga because it helps a great deal to have a prototype in mind as we pursue the ways and means to advance toward city transformation.

The Eight Key Books of the 1990s

The kickoff for this decade of city transformation attempts was John Dawson's book, *Taking Our Cities for God,* which was released in 1989, but which sold 100,000 copies in 1990. Seven other books which, in my estimation, are unusually important followed Dawson's book during the decade. Other books were written as well, but my intent is not to present a complete bibliography. Rather than relegating these eight key books to a small-print footnote, I think it would be well to list them and comment on them here along with my recommendation that, if you want to build a core city transformation library, you acquire them all. I will list them in order of publication:

♦ *Taking Our Cities for God* by John Dawson (Creation House, 1989). This book, more than any other, caused the body of Christ to begin to focus their attention for prayer, spiritual warfare, corporate repentance, and evangelism on their entire city. It was the spark that lit the fire of city taking across the country.

♦ *The House of the Lord: God's Plan to Liberate Your City from Darkness* by Francis Frangipane (Creation House, 1991). In the year before Francis Frangipane wrote this book, the crime rate in the state of Iowa went up 11 percent, while the city of Cedar Rapids, where he was putting city transformation principles to the test, the crime rate dropped 17 percent. This book summarizes what Frangipane learned, especially in the areas of prayer and spiritual warfare.

♦ *That None Should Perish* by Ed Silvoso (Regal Books, 1994). Silvoso's ideas, forged through the fire of revival in Argentina, introduced many new and valuable concepts including "prayer evangelism." In fact, his subtitle is "How to Reach Entire Cities for Christ Through Prayer Evangelism." His main laboratory for applying the principles at that time was the city of Resistencia in northern Argentina, a city which has shown measurable effects of targeting a whole city. Whereas Dawson introduced the term "city taking," Silvoso introduced the term "city reaching."

♦ *Primary Purpose* by Ted Haggard (Creation House, 1995). I love Ted Haggard's subtitle: "Making It Hard for People to Go to Hell From Your City." When Haggard was called from Baker, Louisiana to Colorado Springs in 1985, he clearly interpreted his call as a call to the city, not primarily to a denomination or a local church or another sort of ministry. In the last chapter of this book, I relate some things that have recently happened in Colorado Springs as fruit of Ted's, somewhat atypical, broad-scale vision.

♦ *Loving Your City into the Kingdom: City-Reaching Strategies for a 21st-Century Revival* by Ted Haggard and Jack Hayford (Regal Books, 1997). Two of America's foremost megachurch pastors invited 21 other Christian leaders who had important things to say about city reaching to join them in this amazing collection of ideas and insights. To mention a few, we have Bill Bright, George Barna, Paul Cedar, Jack Dennison, Alice Smith, Joe Aldrich, George Otis,

Jr., David Bryant, and others. This book will be a treasure chest for you.

♦ *Revival! It Can Transform Your City* by C. Peter Wagner (Wagner Publications, 1999). I wrote this book at the end of the 1990s after analyzing the significant progress that we had made since *Taking Our Cities for God* in putting together city transformation initiatives in many cities. In it, I suggest five important things that we need to do or to do better if we expect to see our cities transformed. However, when I wrote it I could only include a couple of paragraphs on apostolic leadership in the city because I didn't know then what I know now. This book picks up where that one left off and examines how recognizing and affirming city apostles might well be the most vital missing link for getting the task done and done well.

♦ *Informed Intercession* by George Otis, Jr. (Renew, 1999). George Otis has done more research on cities in advanced stages of transformation than anyone else. He reports his research to date in this book, and he brilliantly analyzes the strengths and weaknesses of what has been going on. His subtitle, "Transforming Your Community Through Spiritual Mapping and Strategic Prayer" reveals his two-pronged focus. There is no more insightful book on the list than this one, as you will discover. George's term "city transformation" is the one that most leaders in the field have adopted at the present time. Otis' hour-long video, *Transformations*, a documentary of transformations occurring in four cities, is the most motivational resource for city transformation available at this writing.

♦ *City Reaching: On the Road to Community Transformation* by Jack Dennison (William Carey Library, 1999).

No one has actually been working with leaders on the front lines of city transformation in more cities across America during the 1990s than Jack Dennison. This experience, combined with an acutely analytical mind and an ability to organize and present material, has given Jack the basis for this thorough summary of the things that we have learned about structuring the process of city transformation across the board. Jim Herrington of Houston, Texas, contributed two chapters as well. This is a very important textbook.

Four Valid Assumptions

There are four valid assumptions, helped greatly by the above authors, that were worked out largely in the 1990s and which I see as essential for moving forward toward city transformation. I think it is accurate to say that the first three assumptions are now accepted by almost all of those who have personal, ongoing involvement in processes of city transformation. The fourth has been molded and shaped during the 1990s, but it is still new enough so that many leaders have not as yet made up their minds whether they will accept it as valid. Because it is new, I will elaborate on it a bit more than on the other three.

Assumption #1: *The unity of the body of Christ is a prerequisite for city transformation.* We agree that there is not one individual or one church or one parachurch ministry that can successfully carry out a city transformation process all by themselves. Ed Silvoso speaks for many when he says: "The first step in taking a city for Christ is to build—or reestablish—God's perimeter in the city . . . In your city a spiritual beachhead must be established. This is usually done by the coming together of the 'faithful remnant' . . . The remnant must come together not because they have common interests or doctrines but because they share the same life: Jesus. . . . [Jesus'] undershepherds come to meet with Him in order to receive instruction and edification. As a result, everything else becomes secondary and subservient to these endeavors."[1]

Those who preach on this frequently use as a text Ephesians 4:3, "Endeavoring to keep the unity of the Spirit in the bond of peace," or John 17:21, "That they all may be one, as You, Father, are in Me, and I in You; that they also may be one in Us, that the world may believe that You sent Me."

Assumption #2: *The local church pastors are the spiritual gatekeepers of the city.* In terms of spiritual authority, the pastors of the local churches are those who are divinely appointed to the highest ranks. Individual Christians are under the spiritual covering of their pastors. The Bible says, "Obey those who rule over you, and be submissive, for they watch out for your souls, as those who must give account" (Heb. 13:17). Pastors, by the very definition of the term, take responsibility first and foremost for their sheep.

Even in cities where high-visibility leaders may head national and international parachurch ministries, those individuals rarely sense or exercise spiritual authority for the city in which they live. There could be exceptions, but they would be rare.

In some cities, laypeople across denominational boundaries often sense and live out more unity than their pastors do. The unity of laypeople is commendable, but it is never as powerful a base for city transformation as the unity of the pastors. The reason is that the pastors, not the laypeople, are the city's spiritual gatekeepers.

Assumption #3: *The church of the city is spiritually one church with multiple congregations.* Back in the first century, all congregations of believers were house churches. There was no such thing as a church building. All the believers of a given city did not meet together once a week to hear the same sermon. Nevertheless, when Paul wrote to the believers in Corinth, for example, he said, "To the church of God which is at Corinth," (2 Cor. 1:1), using "church" in the singular. In Paul's mind, he was writing to the church of the city.

Ed Silvoso says, "The faithful remnant must hold firm to two foundational principles: they believe God for the city, and there is only one Church in the city, although it meets in many congregations."[2] Francis Frangipane says, "It takes a citywide church to win a citywide war."[3] Few church leaders today would disagree with Silvoso and Frangipane.

Assumption # 4: *The foundation of the church is apostles and prophets.* Stated so plainly, this assumption may seem like a truism. One of the reasons is that it brings to mind Ephesians 2:20, "[The household of God is] built on the foundation of the apostles and prophets, Jesus Christ Himself being the chief cornerstone." Some will say, "Isn't this what everyone knows that the Bible teaches?"

It is, but some, when they read it, assume that the apostles and prophets got the church started in the first century, and when that task was completed and the canon of Scripture was closed, there was no more need for apostles and prophets in the church. However, they would do well to realize that the same book of Ephesians goes on to say that we still need apostles and prophets. It says that when Jesus ascended into heaven, "[He] gave gifts to men" (Eph. 4:8). What were these gifts? "He Himself gave some to be *apostles*, some *prophets*, some evangelists, and some pastors and teachers" (Eph. 4:11, emphasis mine).

Generally speaking, we have been comfortable with evangelists, pastors, and teachers in our churches. But some have had a serious problem with apostles and prophets. There is, however, little justification for drawing an imaginary exegetical line between the first two offices and the latter three in the same verse. Apostles and prophets belong there, but for how long? "Till we all come to the unity of the faith and the knowledge of the Son of God, to a perfect man, to the measure of the stature of the fullness of Christ" (Eph. 4:12). I don't know anyone who would say that the church as we know it has reached this stage of unity and perfection. Therefore, it seems, we still need apostles and prophets.

Apostles of the City

A church without active apostles and prophets is a church with an incomplete foundation. The Bible does not say that this foundation is "elders" or "shepherd leaders" or "men of peace" or "facilitators" or "conveners" or "anchor church pastors," to cite some of the terms currently used by those who are seeking handles on how to bring effective city transformation leadership together.

My point is that, if the church of the city is truly one church, as the accepted opinion of Christian leaders would have it, the foundation of that church, as well as the individual local churches and denominations and apostolic networks, is, biblically speaking, apostles and prophets.

I am writing this book because the existing literature on city transformation that I have seen does not deal directly with this crucial point. Let me clarify that in this book I am stressing *apostles* of the city, not *prophets* of the city. I actually deal with the subject of the relationship of apostles and prophets in my recent book, *Apostles and Prophets: The Foundation of the Church* (Regal Books), but there I do not address the concept of city apostles. These two books compliment each other.

Frustration Has Set In

The decade of the 1990s has set in place some extremely important assumptions about city transformation. But as I talk to leaders across the country, I am perceiving a growing sense of frustration. These are good ideas that we are applying to our cities. They are biblical. They glorify God. Corporately we are in a much better place as a church than we were ten years ago, and we can praise God together for that!

Let's analyze our city transformation experiments to date. There are not just a few of them. Multiple attempts at seeing change in our cities can be cataloged in just about all 50 states. But the tough question is: *Have these experiments been successful or unsuccessful?*

My best answer to that question is that, yes, we have had a number of successes, but short-term successes by and large. Over the long haul, city after city reports strenuous efforts, but these efforts are producing few measurable indicators that cities are literally being transformed in the way that we have desired for more than ten years.

A simple conclusion is that there must be some flaws in what we have been doing. In my opinion, there are two principal flaws: (1) Our model for structuring city transformation is flawed, and (2) Our citywide leadership selection design is flawed. I will deal with them one at a time in the next two chapters.

Notes
1. Ed Silvoso, *That None Should Perish* (Ventura CA: Regal Books, 1994), pp. 218, 222
2. Ibid., p. 228
3. Francis Frangipane, *The House of the Lord* (Lake Mary FL: Creation House, 1991), p. 152.

CHAPTER TWO

OUR MODEL IS FLAWED

The first flaw that I suspect may be causing considerable frustration in efforts toward city transformation, is the citywide model that we usually adopt for the process. It will not take long to explain this, so this chapter will be quite short.

The Model

Cooperation among churches in a given American city is nothing new. In city after city, we have been doing it for years. For the last 40-50 years, the cooperative model most common in our cities has been the Billy Graham evangelistic campaign. I'm using the name "Billy Graham" because that can be considered almost a generic term for citywide evangelistic programs. There are many other public evangelists who go from city to city, but almost all of them follow the pattern first established in the 1950s by the Billy Graham Evangelistic Association.

It seems that one thing a wide variety of churches can agree upon is the need to evangelize the lost people of a city. Almost all pastors agree that there is virtually nothing for their church to lose by cooperating with other churches to invite a high-profile evangelist like Billy Graham or Luis Palau or Greg Laurie to come to the city for a few days. Whether or not cooperating churches, through the years, have typically burst into new and vigorous conversion growth as an outcome of citywide evangelism does not seem to be a major consideration. There is one thing for sure that will happen: a highly visible media event will take place which will draw the attention of the general public and which will provide a deep sense of satisfaction to all those who participate. After all, Billy Graham was the seventh most admired figure of the 20th Century, and associating with him could only produce a positive outcome.

The major reason that cities continued to use the Billy Graham committee as our principal model throughout the 1900s was very simple. It was the only viable and proven model that we had!

The Billy Graham Committee Works!

Why has the Billy Graham committee model endured for 40-50 years? The only factor that would perpetuate it for so long is that people all over have found out that it works!

That is to say, it works for its purpose. When a Billy Graham campaign comes to a city, the process usually produces a very broad and diverse sponsoring committee. The typical Billy Graham citywide committee brings together pastors and top lay leaders across denominational, racial, and social class lines in a remarkable way. A notably high percentage of the pastors of the city choose to cooperate. Many cities look back to their citywide evangelistic initiative with amazement, because after it was over they could never again seem to generate such unity of the body of Christ. It was a mountaintop experience for them.

Why Does This Model Work?

Now let's look at this Billy Graham committee a bit more closely and ask the crucial question: Why does it work so well?

It works well because it has the two principal ingredients to make any such effort successful, namely leadership and a united vision. But it is very important to understand that both the leadership and the vision come from outside of the city. The Billy Graham Evangelistic Association (BGEA) has a long track record of successfully uniting the Christian leadership of a city for a public evangelistic campaign. They know by experience what should be done and what should not be done. They know the sequence of organization and the proper timing. They have certain predetermined policies. Every new city is not allowed to reinvent the wheel. Representatives of the BGEA monitor the process and make sure that everything is going along according to plan.

When all the work is done and everything is ready, the chairperson of the board, so to speak, comes in from the outside and speaks to the people of the city for a number of nights and in certain events scheduled during the daytime. The local and regional newspapers, television, and radio feature the occasion.

The Result

What is the result? Keep in mind that I am not asking about the *evangelistic* results. That is another subject which I have dealt with in books such as *Strategies for Church Growth* (Regal Books). Here I am discussing the Billy Graham pattern as the model for citywide Christian events with which we have become the most accustomed.

Notice that the large number of pastors and other Christian leaders of the city who are enlisted for the sponsoring committee have become the *supporting cast* for the public ministry of the outside evangelist. This is fine. It is what they are supposed to do. That is what they have signed up for. But the very design of this model will not allow the sponsoring committee to generate its own initiating, visionary leadership to plan and execute the event. Once invited to the city, the Billy Graham Evangelistic Association casts the overall vision, sets in place the operational design, and the pastors and other Christian leaders generate the funding and help make it happen.

Part of the design is that certain individuals from the city will be recognized as leaders of the sponsoring committee, and they will be the ones who work most closely with the representatives of the Billy Graham Evangelistic Association. They will convene and chair the committee and the subcommittee meetings. They will get to sit on the platform with Billy Graham when he arrives. Some of them will be asked to lead in prayer or read Scripture or make public announcements or introduce the mayor or serve as master of ceremonies. They will be invited to the press conferences.

These individuals who come to be designated as leaders of the citywide sponsoring committee find that their role is mostly diplomatic and administrative. They typically are bridge-builders and peacekeepers. Their roster usually does not include the more controversial figures who sometimes are seen by others as coloring outside the lines or upsetting the status quo.

The Flaw

As I have said, this model for citywide cooperation works. But it can and does work for *one event*. The flaw of this model is that, for *city transformation,* a radical switch needs to be made in at least three areas:

♦ We have to switch from *outside leadership* to *inside leadership.* The initiation and the vision for city transformation must come from those who are already in the city and committed to the city. Outside resources are fine, but they must now be the supporting cast, not the core leadership.

♦ We have to switch from *event-orientation* to *process-orientation.* It is one thing to work together for weeks or months in order to facilitate one climactic event such as a citywide evangelistic campaign. It is another thing to organize the Christian leadership of the city in an ongoing process of transformation which will remain in place for the long haul year after year.

♦ We have to switch from *diplomatic and administrative leaders* to *aggressive, initiating, risk-taking leaders.*

This last point, in my opinion, is the most crucial of all. It leads us into the next chapter in which I want to attempt to explain how we can and must make this leadership switch.

—————◆—————

CHAPTER THREE

OUR LEADERSHIP SELECTION DESIGN IS FLAWED

Let's say we agree that for spearheading an effective city transformation initiative we need inside, process-oriented, initiating and vision-casting leadership. If we can agree on that, then the next question becomes: How do we get this kind of leadership in place?

My contention, and my incentive for writing this book, is that we have tried to get this kind of leadership in place for years, but we haven't been as successful as we might want to be. We usually begin by recognizing that the local church pastors are the spiritual gatekeepers of the city. We move on from there, using the model that we learned from the Billy Graham Evangelistic Association, and we form a citywide committee of as many pastors as we can convene. We begin to meet on a regular basis, usually every month. Our expectation is that the necessary visionary, initiating leadership to inspire and guide the transformation of our city will surface from within this group.

But such a thing has not materialized in very many cases. My conclusion, therefore, would be that somehow the design that we have been using to find and set these leaders in place must be flawed.

Why hasn't it worked that well? Where could the flaw be?

Two Good Ideas
Have Been Overplayed

I think that the first reason why we do not usually end up having the right leaders in place is because we have overplayed two good ideas. At the outset, I need to affirm the validity of both of these ideas. They are biblical. They have a crucial place in the process of city transformation. They invariably produce much personal satisfaction on the part of the pastors and other leaders involved. I am in favor of both of these ideas.

But, having said that, let me also say as clearly as I can that if these two ideas become *determinative* for the whole city transformation process, they will likely *inhibit* rather than *stimulate* the emergence of visionary leadership. These ideas are like salt. Sometimes I make a salad, taste a sample, and say, "Oh! I forgot the salt!" Without the salt it tastes blah. Then I sprinkle on some salt, taste it again, and it is wonderful! Everyone who cooks has experienced the same thing. But also everyone who cooks knows that if I keep shaking and shaking the salt and get too much of it, the salad becomes inedible.

The tendency in our cities has been to oversalt our process with these two good and necessary ideas. When we do, I would not go so far as to label these ideas *dysfunctional*, but I would simply say that they eventually become *nonfunctional*. "Nonfunctional" is a polysyllabic word meaning that they don't work.

What are these two ideas?

The Concept of the "City Church"

At its root, as I explained in Chapter 1, the idea that there is one church of the city and that it meets in different congregations is biblically and experientially sound. But there is more than one way of understanding and applying the concept. In the next chapter I come back to this idea and I try to show how it can be fruitfully applied to our city taking designs.

But, meanwhile, the most common expression that I have heard pastors repeat, as if by rote, is: "We are the church of the city and we are all co-pastors of different congregations." This sounds so humble and so self-effacing and so much like the fruit of the Spirit that it appears to be beyond discussion. However, it introduces a subtle but serious flaw into the leadership selection design. If we affirm that we are all co-pastors we enter into an egalitarian mindset which will inevitably erect a barrier against the possibility of recognizing strong leadership. To reverse a common saying, we are all Indians with no chief!

The Pastors' Prayer Summits

The second good idea which, when overplayed, can inhibit the emergence of strong citywide leadership is the Pastors' Prayer Summit. Without question, Pastors' Prayer Summits have gone down in the records as one of the spiritual highlights of the 1990s in cities across America. Birthed by Joe

Aldrich of Multnomah School of the Bible, summits have been attended at least once, and sometimes repeated times, by clergy of all denominations.

The concept is that pastors from all over the city would go away together for three or four days to meet with God. That was the only declared purpose. The focus was to be on God. He would be the one to direct the proceedings day after day. A classic prayer summit would have no leaders, no agenda, no speakers, no song leaders, no announcements, just an expectation that God would be in charge.

One of the reasons that prayer summits swept the country for years and are still popular in some places is that those who attend usually testify afterwards that it was a mountaintop spiritual experience for them. Large numbers of pastors achieved unity of heart with one another; they repented to each other and entered into mutual forgiveness. Many pastors experienced personal spiritual renewal that has been ongoing. Some of their churches caught the afterglow of the experience and entered into congregational renewal. A new level of unity was achieved among church leaders in many American cities.

What flaw could possibly surface in a wonderful experience like a Pastor's Prayer Summit? There is no flaw in the experience. The problem emerges, however, when the prayer summit, after one or two successful occurrences, then becomes the major ongoing vehicle for achieving and sustaining unity in a given city, as it has in some cities. Since an agenda is not allowed, it is not possible for visionary, initiating citywide leaders to surface in a prayer summit. There is little compelling drive to do whatever it takes to forge a united vision for the transformation of the city.

United prayer can and does have its own inherent benefits. But unless united prayer centers around united vision, i.e., an agenda, it will not go far for city transformation.

Counterproductive Leadership Selection

Overplaying the two good ideas of the church of the city and the Pastors' Prayer Summits constitute the first reason why we have not generally seen the emergence of the leadership that we need for city transformation. The second reason, in my way of seeing things, is that our operational dynamics for leadership selection have turned out to be counterproductive.

If this suspicion is correct, it is extremely important— perhaps more important than some might think at first glance. As I have mentioned, George Otis, Jr. is the foremost researcher of cities in advanced stages of transformation. Before he wrote his book, *Informed Intercession*, he had investigated eighteen cities in different parts of the world in considerable depth, only one of which was in the United States. His observations showed that there were at least five commonalities that surfaced as a cross-cultural pattern through most of the eighteen cities. Two of the five were present in *all* of the eighteen. The first on the list? "Persevering leadership."[1] While other elements such as prayer and unity and repentance are extremely important for city transformation, without the right leadership in place they will not be able to bear their expected fruit.

The Value of Relationships

One significant advance through the decade of the 1990s was a growing consensus that meaningful, productive unity will stand or fall based on the personal relationships among leaders. Pastors' Prayer Summits have done an admirable job of helping church leaders to establish and reestablish these valuable personal relationships.

A generation ago it was different. Unity was generally perceived as best being promoted through organizations such as city ministeriums which would typically have constitutions, bylaws, members, dues, elected officers, regular meetings, treasuries, and the like. Our present generation, which some refer to as "post-modern," does not track that well with organizational or bureaucratic bases for unity. Personal relationships are what matter the most. Most of the city transformation efforts that I have been in touch with understand this, and they are operating on the assumption that leadership emerges from productive relationships.

Problem No. 1:
Relationships Have Limitations

I have mentioned this because, as I see it, the first problem that has emerged in leadership selection in our cities relates to a fervent desire among some pastors to establish and build large numbers of personal relationships across as diverse a spectrum as possible. This, of course, is commendable. But consider the fact that the energy required for building personal relationships across unfamiliar social, racial, denominational, cultural, theological, and church-size lines is extremely demanding.   If this is allowed to become a determinative factor in building an infrastructure for city transformation, it can turn out to be counterproductive.

By this, I am not saying that it cannot or that it should not be done. It can be done because the fruit of the Holy Spirit is present in the lives of most church leaders. In fact, in some places it has been done to a point through prayer summits and regular gatherings of pastors of a city. I have heard of pastors who have resolved to be best friends with at least one other pastor with whom personal relationships would not be natural. For instance, an African-American pastor may resolve to become best friends with a Korean pastor. A suburban pastor may resolve to become best friends with an inner-city pastor. A megachurch pastor may resolve to become best friends with a pastor who has never broken the 200 barrier. An Assemblies of God pastor may resolve to become best friends with a Lutheran pastor. An urban pastor may resolve to become best friends with a rural pastor. A charismatic pastor may resolve to become best friends with a cessationist pastor.

All of the above are doable. Many baby boomer pastors, strongly influenced by the social upheavals beginning in the 1960s, have an especially high need for these kinds of relationships. A few of these attempts have actually succeeded. Most of them, however, report promising beginnings, but relatively short lives. In most cases the major issue, as I analyze

---

While other elements such as prayer and unity and repentance are extremely important for city transformation, without the right leadership in place they will not bear their expected fruit.

---

it, is not pride or egoism or racism or carnality or snobbishness, but, pure and simple, energy. If it takes an extraordinary amount of personal energy and discipline to build just one relationship of this sort, it would follow that attempting to build multiple such relationships is no more possible than it is for most humans to run ten miles every day.

Whereas few city transformation efforts have succeeded in making their monthly pastors gatherings reflect the diversity that I have just mentioned, the Billy Graham committee generally can pull it off. Why? It is because the Billy Graham committee is a temporary, event-oriented committee. But over the long haul, even though white pastors, for example, may have a true heart desire to include African-American pastors in their gatherings, and African-American pastors may have a true heart desire to include white pastors in their gatherings, rare is the city where it actually happens. In most American cities this continues to be an ongoing point of frustration.

Actually, according to group dynamic theory, the most productive situation for initiating and nurturing personal relationships is frequent meetings of a group of two to eight persons. As the group grows larger, especially passing 12 and then 17, it becomes more and more difficult to develop much of anything beyond superficial relationships. A monthly meeting of 40 or 60 pastors will not do it, even over a year's time. But many cities have been expecting it to happen with meetings this size.

Problem No. 2:
Unity Can Become an End in Itself

Let's say that the effort for establishing good relationships across a wide diversity of pastors and church leaders does succeed to a point, as it has in some cities. The danger here becomes that a new syndrome is frequently initiated. Our new, very satisfying relationships are reported as "true renewal" or "a powerful God-thing" that must be nurtured and sustained at all costs. The perception subtly arises that if our cordial, monthly meetings can only be sustained, they will turn out to be an unstoppable launching pad for city transformation.

In other words, unity can, and sometimes does, become an end in itself! "Behold, how good and how pleasant it is for brethren to dwell together in unity!" (Psalm 133:1). When this happens, unity, not necessarily city transformation, becomes the primary goal of the group. If our city is transformed, fine, but if it is not we still have our precious unity.

A Weakness of Citywide Evangelism

It might be worth mentioning in passing that this very syndrome has arisen in many citywide evangelistic campaigns. Research has shown that, across the board, the number of those who make first-time decisions for Christ at a citywide evangelistic campaign and who subsequently become responsible members of local churches runs between 3 percent and 16 percent. While I am thankful for each one who is saved, I feel that this percentage is lower than it needs to be. The phenomenon of unity becoming an end in itself during the preparation for the campaign has been a chief contributing factor toward the low percentage.

Some may wonder how anyone can complain about too much unity. First of all, let me respond by pointing out that one of the chief passages in the Bible for those who advocate unlimited Christian unity, John 17:21, carefully avoids allowing unity to become an end in itself. The unity there is a means toward another end, namely that lost people will be saved. "That they all may be one, as You, Father, are in Me, and I in You; that they also may be one in Us, *that the world may believe that You sent Me*" (emphasis mine). Understanding this helps avoid an inflated application of John 17.

It is also interesting to note that throughout church history the great, dramatic movements of God rarely, if ever, began as the consequence of conscious efforts to stimulate and preserve Christian unity. Most of them were, in fact, born out of quite serious division in the body of Christ. Jesus said that He did not come to bring peace, but a sword (see Matt. 10:34). If this seems strange, ask Martin Luther or John Wesley or John Knox or William Booth. In the eighteen cities in advanced stages of transformation that George Otis, Jr. has researched, none of the transformation movements was born out of a context of previously planned and executed citywide Christian unity. The fact of the matter is that unity has more often than not come about as a *result* of city transformation rather than as a *cause* of city transformation.

Problem No. 3:
Courtesy Trumps Conviction

If the unity card is overplayed, courtesy can very easily trump conviction, as I have heard George Otis, Jr. say.

In some of the groups of leaders which have been developing in our cities, a somewhat predictable set of clichés develops. I have often heard and read phrases such as "unconditional love," "deference to one another," "regarding others more highly than yourself," "nameless and faceless people," or "no superstars." When these kinds of concepts become the guiding principles, the outcome is that the group will inexorably gravitate toward the least common denominator.

What does this least common denominator look like?

While there are undoubtedly some notable exceptions, generally speaking the group meeting regularly and advocating city transformation is traditional, white, middle class, Republican, denominational evangelicalism.

The Trade-off

What are the requirements for active participation in the group? Since courtesy tends to trump conviction, an interesting trade-off occurs:

- ♦ Evangelicals, in order to participate in the group, are not required to give up any of their traditional evangelical distinctives except a bit of residual cessationism on the part of some.
- ♦ Charismatics, in order to participate in the group, must leave their major distinctives at the door. As the group meets together, there is, more often than not, no room for tongues, prophecy, concert prayer, extravagant body language, high volume, travail in intercession or intense and prolonged worship.

At this point a bit of drop off begins to occur. Some charismatic pastors may begin to attend less regularly. There is rarely any comment about this rather unfair trade-off expressed either verbally or in writing because the rule of courtesy prevails. Many former participants simply vaporize, so to speak.

The bottom line question then becomes: What kind of leadership emerges from this least-common-denominator group of pastors? Almost inevitably we find ourselves with affirming, consensus-building, peace-loving, maintenance-oriented leadership. The objective of such leaders is to preserve the status quo in the most stimulating way possible! Is this the kind of leadership that is likely to spearhead an aggressive, bold, powerful movement that will literally shake a city?

Problem No. 4:
Certain Key Pastors
Decide to Self-Exclude

The kind of group I have just described will invariably cause some key pastors of the city to self-exclude. These are fairly prominent pastors who have been invited, even at times cajoled, to participate. They often show up at first, then they find reasons to turn down repeated invitations.

Who are the key pastors who tend to self-exclude from many of our current groups of church leaders dedicated to city transformation? They fall into at least six recognizable categories:

1. Vision-driven pastors. Vision-driven pastors are usually restless with patching up old wineskins and preserving the status quo. What turns them on is breaking new ground, especially if some traditionalists may get shaken up in the process.
2. Task-oriented pastors. Task-oriented pastors are among the first to see what I have explained above, namely that prioritizing unity will not get the job of city transformation done. They are driven by the kind of consecrated pragmatism which does not necessarily shy away from pushing others around a bit if that is a requirement for reaching their goals.
3. Growing megachurch pastors. By using this phrase, I am referring to pastors of megachurches that are not

plateaued or declining, but that continue to be dynamic and growing. That is an important distinction. These pastors of growing megachurches typically have an agenda problem. The agenda that motivates them day by day and week by week is in another solar system when compared to the agendas of typical maintenance-oriented leaders of city taking groups.

4. Charismatic pastors. I have already mentioned some charismatic pastors who lose interest when their distinctives are excluded from the group. But other charismatic pastors who may not be that sensitive about their distinctives are simply bored with the meetings. A high-visibility charismatic pastor once told me that he decided to attend a prayer summit that was to meet for three days. He said, "Peter, to me the first hour was the equivalent of three days!"

5. Apostles. Experienced apostles are very much aware of apostolic spheres. When they begin to attend the city transformation meetings, many of them immediately sense that they are outside of their sphere, and they know that their gift of apostle thereby becomes virtually inoperative. Since their time is limited, they often choose to spend their time in situations where the anointing they have in their own spheres is operative.

6. Influential ethnic leaders. While in most cities that I am aware of, a number of good-hearted, bridge-building ethnic leaders actively participate in the city transformation group, usually the pastors who are the movers and shakers within their nuclear ethnic group do not show up. A certain cultural gap often raises a glass wall. For a starter, most ethnic leaders, especially in the inner city, are Democrats!

Why Don't They Continue?

A good many of the pastors who would find themselves in one or more of the above groups actually show up when the citywide meetings are first called. They are often motivated by a guilty conscience and a feeling of obligation. They know that they would participate in a Billy Graham committee because at least that committee has leadership and vision for a task, so they give this group a try, even though neither their hearts nor their minds are really in it. But soon the reality sets in. They have other priorities which cause them to attend less frequently and then drop out.

When they drop out, the whispering starts. Participating pastors begin asking each other: "Why don't they continue?" I have heard all of these responses to that question:

- ♦ "They are indifferent to the city."
- ♦ "They just go around tooting their own horn."
- ♦ 'They are on an ego trip."
- ♦ "They are a bunch of empire builders."
- ♦ "They really didn't want to cooperate with us in the first place."
- ♦ "They need to deal with their pride."
- ♦ "They don't believe in the church of the city."
- ♦ "If they don't lead it, they don't join it."

Consider that last phrase: "If they don't lead it, they don't join it." That, as a matter of fact, is very true. The reason that they don't join it if they can't lead it is very simple. They are, first and foremost, *leaders*. What do leaders do? They lead! To ask them to join something they can't lead is like asking a singer to join a choir, but not letting him or her sing. If you are a singer, you have to sing. If you are a leader, you have to lead.

The dilemma that this causes is the ones who self-exclude from the process are precisely the ones who have the necessary giftedness, anointing, and ability to lead a successful city transformation initiative.

The result? The system settles for mediocre leadership and filters out the most creative leadership. That is why I contend that our leadership selection design for city transformation is flawed.

So much for the analysis of why such a great deal of frustration has set in after ten years of sincerely trying to organize pastors and other church leaders for city transformation. If that is the diagnosis, let's now turn to the cure.

Notes
1. George Otis, Jr., *Informed Intercession* (Ventura CA: Renew, 1999), p. 56.

CHAPTER FOUR

APOSTLES OF THE CITY

How, then, can we begin to move into a more functional and productive future for the actual transformation of our cities?

Three Crucial Concepts

As a starter, I believe that we need to acknowledge, understand, and build our future as much as possible on three crucial concepts that might be a bit new to some of us. I have participated in enough rather innovative projects over the course of more than four decades of ministry to help me understand quite well what social scientists call "diffusion of innovation theory." That means that, when innovators propose a new idea, some early adopters accept it quickly, then after a while middle adopters get on board, and finally late adopters decide that it might be a worthwhile idea. All this can be stretched out over a long period of time.

My admonition is that we, as the people of God, should not allow this time line for innovation to stretch out as far as it often does. I do not interpret our mandate as praying that our cities will be transformed 40, 50, or 60 years from now. I would like to see it happening in our generation, not in the next generation. We already have a ten-year head start. As I have been pointing out, we have come a long way. There are some flaws that have surfaced, to be sure, but they are not fatal. The three crucial concepts that I am explaining in this chapter will allow us to correct the flaws and lay the proper groundwork for city transformation. They are: (1) apostles of the city; (2) territorial commitment; and (3) extra-denominational alignments.

Apostles of the City

Some may have observed that I am using "Apostles of the City" as the title for this section, the title for this chapter, and the title for the whole book. I do this intentionally because I want to leave as little room as possible for doubting that I consider this the most crucial new ingredient that we must add to our recipe for city transformation.

There are two conceptual hurdles that many of us will have to jump in order to run on this track. The first hurdle is accepting the validity of the contemporary office of apostle. The second hurdle is understanding how apostles, whom we usually think of as apostles of the *church*, can be apostles of a given *city*.

In Chapter 1, I dealt briefly with the first hurdle, arguing that we should take literally what Ephesians 2:20 says: "[The household of God is] built on the foundation of the apostles and prophets, Jesus Christ Himself being the chief cornerstone." Apostles and prophets are not some historical cameo of a couple of thousand or more years in the past. They are a present day reality. It is extremely important to set this biblical principle in our minds at the outset.

The second hurdle, which I also mentioned in passing in Chapter 1, is that some apostles are apostles of the city. This begins with a principle that fell into the category of "innovative" a few years ago, but which is now generally accepted, namely that the church of the city is one church meeting in many different congregations. Jesus is the great shepherd of the church of the city, and the local church pastors are the undershepherds.

If we can accept the idea that there is a church of the city, and if we recognize that apostles and prophets are the foundation of the church, it follows logically that the city church, as a church, must have apostles. Prophets are something else which I will deal with elsewhere. Therefore, the term "apostles of the city" begins to come into focus.

Apostolic Spheres

Before I draw this to a conclusion and attempt some applications, it will be important to think a bit about apostolic spheres. This is very important to me because, as I go along, I am going to argue that in most cities, particularly in cities with a population over 5,000, there will probably not be just one apostle of the city, but several, each with his or her own sphere.

In First Corinthians, Paul says: "Am I not an apostle? Am I not free? Have I not seen Jesus Christ our Lord? Are you not my work in the Lord? *If I am not an apostle to others, yet doubtless I am to you*" (1 Cor. 9:1-2, emphasis mine). What is Paul affirming here? He is saying, apparently, that he is not an apostle over the whole church everywhere. And such was the case. Paul was not an apostle of Jerusalem or of Rome or of Alexandria. These were not his assigned apostolic spheres. But Corinth certainly was, as was Philippi and Ephesus and Lystra and Crete and other places.

By the time he writes Second Corinthians, Paul is ready to elaborate a bit more on the matter of apostolic spheres. Chapter 10 has more detail on this than any other part of the Bible. He says, "We, however, will not boast beyond measure, but within the limits of the *sphere* which God appointed us—a *sphere* which especially includes you" (2 Cor. 10:13, emphasis mine). Recognizing that apostolic ministry is not effective outside of the designated spheres, Paul goes on to write, "For we are not extending ourselves beyond our sphere" (2 Cor. 10:14). Then when he suggested that he would go to the "re-

---

Here is the bottom line:
If the apostles *of* the city are not
recognized and empowered to lead
as God has anointed them to do,
the divine government of the city will not
be in its proper place.

---

gions beyond," he said that he would avoid "another man's sphere of accomplishment" (2 Cor. 10:16); and that he would not "build on another man's foundation" (Rom 15:20).

I mentioned apostolic spheres briefly in the last chapter when I was trying to explain why some apostles who live in the city would have a tendency to self-exclude from many of the models of citywide committees for city transformation that we have been using over the past ten years. In that group they find themselves out of their own appointed sphere.

I think that there are at least three kinds of apostolic spheres. The most common are *ecclesiastical* spheres in which a certain apostle has authority over a certain cluster of churches. Then there are *functional* spheres in which the apostle is not over certain churches, but over individuals who have a certain type of ministry. And there are also *territorial* spheres in which an apostle will have authority over a certain segment of God's people in a particular geographical area. Obviously it is this last kind of sphere which would include what I am calling "apostles of the city."

Apostles *in* the City and Apostles *of* the City

The preposition *of* is very important. This is why. Living in a city of a decent size there may be a number of apostles. All of these would be apostles *in* the city. But out of them all, in most cases only a few may turn out to be apostles *of* the city. I can use myself as an example. I am recognized by many as an apostle, and I live in Colorado Springs. As far as Colorado Springs is concerned, I am an apostle *in* the city, but I am not an apostle *of* the city.

Here is the bottom line: If the apostles *of* the city are not recognized and empowered to lead as God has anointed them to do, the divine government of the city will not be in its proper place. This can retard the transformation process, and it can cause the nagging frustration that has been characteristic of so many of our cities in recent years. Here is a theological thought on what is happening in such a case. God may desire to move in miraculous ways to transform a city, but He may not be willing to release the process until the apostles are in place.

Why? Because without the proper foundation, revival can be short lived.

If this is the case, the plus side of the concept of the church of the city comes into focus. I mentioned that the negative side was the cliché that "the church of the city meets in many congregations and we are all co-pastors." It is much better not to think that we are all "co-pastors," but rather that the apostles of the city function as senior pastors, each one in their own sphere, and the other pastors in the city function under the apostles as church staff members would ordinarily function under their senior pastor. This is a design that will work!

Territorial Commitment

If the first crucial concept for city transformation is apostles of the city, the second is territorial commitment. I am aware of only one textbook so far on territorial commitment, and that is *Commitment to Conquer* (Chosen Books) by Bob Beckett. In my opinion, Beckett's book is one of the ten most important books of the 1990s. In it, he makes a convincing case for territorial commitment on the part of pastors as a plat-form for spiritual authority in the city. In other words there is usually a direct ratio between the degree of territorial com-mitment and the authority that a given pastor enjoys in the city.

In his book, Bob Beckett tells how for years very little was going right in the church he planted, The Dwelling Place, in Hemet, California. Then, in a supernatural way, God spoke to him about committing himself and his family to Hemet. He and his wife, Susan, purchased cemetery plots, and one Sunday they announced to the congregation that this is where

God had called them for the rest of their lives. The dramatic changes in the church and in the community from that moment are thoroughly documented. In fact, Hemet is one of the four cities in advanced stages of transformation that George Otis, Jr. features in his remarkable video, *Transformations.*

Not all pastors are like Bob Beckett. Even though it is obvious when you think about it, some readers will be surprised at the following statement: 90 percent of American pastors do not expect to be in their same church ten years from now! What I am saying is that, generally speaking, American pastors have very little built-in territorial commitment. The average pastoral tenure among Southern Baptists, our largest denomination, is 2.7 years. The average among our second largest denomination, United Methodists, is 3.4 years. Christian churches average 18 months and The Church of God, Cleveland, averages 2.5 years, just to cite some well-known examples. Very few pastors who change parishes that frequently will be looked upon as apostles of the city.

Who, then, will be the apostles of the city? They will likely be found among those Christian leaders who have literally committed their lives, their families' lives, and their ministries to the city. I have a hard time understanding why more pastors are not like dentists or attorneys or law enforcement officers or general contractors or teachers or automobile dealers—most of them plan to be in the same city the rest of their lives. If such were the case with pastors, they would have more territorial authority.

Megachurch Pastors

I think that some parachurch ministry leaders may be true apostles of the city. But they undoubtedly would be the exception, not the rule. The rule is that local church pastors would most likely be apostles of the city because, as we have pointed out, they are the spiritual gatekeepers of the city. But out of all the local church pastors in a city, the most likely segment among them to be seen as a pool for identifying apostles of the city would be megachurch pastors.

Why would this be? Here is an axiom: The larger the church the longer the pastoral tenure. Few megachurch pastors ever move or ever plan to move. They fully expect to be in their same parishes ten years or twenty years or more from now. Even denominational pastors have a pattern of being transferred frequently when their churches are small, but when they get their promotions to the largest churches in the district or the association or the synod, they move much more infrequently. In other words, pastors of larger churches tend to have more territorial commitment.

The Megachurch Pastor "Issue"

I have a hard time understanding why some Christian leaders persist in making an "issue" of megachurch pastors, as if they were the bad guys in the kingdom of God. After all, their churches have not grown to 2,000 or 3,000 or 10,000 or 20,000 by mere happenstance. While it may be true that there are occasional rogues and scoundrels among them, the rule is that megachurch pastors are extraordinary individuals who not only know principles of leadership and church growth, but who also have received a special divine anointing to apply what they know and to open doors for their members to be all that God wants them to be.

Here is a rather amazing observation about megachurches from the famous management consultant, Peter Drucker:

"Consider the pastoral megachurches that have been growing so very fast in the U.S. since 1980 and are surely the most important social phenomenon in American society in the last 30 years."[1]   John Vaughan, author of *Megachurches and America's Cities,* says, "The time has come to cease the creation of false guilt and blame for growth that leads to larger churches. . . God will not apologize for the growth he provided for his churches and neither should we."[2]

Some people deeply involved in traditional models for city transformation have become quite upset with megachurch pastors because they don't seem to cooperate as actively as some might hope with the associations of churches that are being set up in the cities. I have heard some say that megachurches do not lend themselves to catalyze city transformation processes. Some argue that megachurches are not really needed, implying that the smaller churches in the city can and should transform the city on their own. One whom I have heard even accuses megachurches of being oblivious to the rest of the body of Christ.

Fine-Tuning Our Structures

The fact of the matter is that we can find considerable truth in some of these observations. But there are two ways of responding to such a state of affairs. One is to write off megachurch pastors as viable, front-line, initiating participants in the city transformation process. This, unfortunately, has been the most frequent response. The other, which is much more preferable, is to fine-tune our city reaching structures so that megachurch pastors will enthusiastically join ranks and put their capable shoulders to the wheel.

One city transformation leader affirms the need to include megachurch pastors in the leadership group, but he laments that they cannot do it because they don't have the time. So he invites them to be on an advisory team. The only reason why the megachurch pastors whom I know would consent to be on an advisory team would be that they see it as the most courteous way of dealing with the fact that they do not want to be a part of the leadership team, which is usually a least-common-denominator group. And their time available? Most megachurch pastors, because of their ability to lead their church while delegating the management responsibilities to a multi-member staff, have enormous amounts of discretionary time at their disposal. They usually have plenty of time to do whatever they feel is important for them to do. The city transformation meetings do not ordinarily occupy a high position on their priority lists.

Pastor Ted Haggard sees the picture clearly. He says, "The biggest church in town often doesn't even participate in the network of churches, either because they weren't invited or because they believe the network is too inactive in terms of citywide strategy. In the coming years this will change. Megachurches will initiate relationships with other churches in the city, and more local churches will begin to turn to the megachurch leaders, who are often proactive and visionary, to develop a citywide strategy."[3]

The Hypothesis of "Pastor-Apostles"

This is just a hypothesis at the moment, but if it is eventually proven to have validity, it would reinforce my contention that one of the most promising pools in which to search for apostles of the city is among pastors of the larger churches. I think that it may well be true that pastors of *dynamic, growing* churches of over 700-800 will almost always have an accompanying gift of apostle. They could be seen as "pastor-apostles." I italicized "*dynamic*" and "*growing*" because pastors of large churches which are stagnant, plateaued, or declining would not ordinarily fit this pattern. Let me explain.

For one thing, churches of 700-800 have about as many people in them as seven or eight average churches in the city. This would constitute a small apostolic network in itself. Megachurches of 5,000 would equal about 50 average congregations. A pastor-pastor or a pastor-teacher who has decent leadership skills can take a church to the 700-800 range, but not far beyond unless the gift of apostle kicks in.

Lyle Schaller says that a church of over 700 should be seen as a "minidenomination,"[4] and that, by definition, would require more than ordinary pastoral leadership if it remains dynamic and growing. Gary McIntosh labels pastoral role changes through different church sizes from worker, skilled worker, lead man, foreman, supervisor, middle management, and top management up to 799. Then he calls 800-1999 "president" and 2,000+ "chairman."[5] In my terminology, the president and the chairman would be pastor-apostles. Churches this size, incidentally, constitute only about 2 percent of American churches.

To summarize this section, let me hasten to say that not all megachurch pastors or not all pastor-apostles are also apostles *of* the city. But it is an excellent place to start looking for them!

Extra-Denominational Alignments

This third crucial concept as a foundation for strategizing city transformation is simply an observation. It is not something that we must work on; it is something that is already happening before our very eyes.

I have said a lot about pastors' groups forming in our cities over the last few years. A very important by-product of this is that, for some of the pastors, the new relationships emerging from these associations are actually stronger than their relationship with pastors in their own denominational structures. It is these new extra-denominational alignments in the city where the focus of friendship, commitment, loyalty, and mutual accountability are the highest for some pastors.

This social phenomenon is so compelling that a number of pastors have even begun to lose interest in attending their regional and national denominational meetings. If this continues to grow, as some predict that it will, it is highly probable that we will begin to see the development of numbers of spontaneous territorial spheres rising to higher importance than traditional denominational affiliations.

As I see it, the multiplication of extra-denominational affiliations provides an ideal social structure for defining apostolic spheres in a city.   How apostles of the city could function effectively in such an environment is projected in the next, and final, chapter.

Notes
[1] Peter F. Drucker, "Management's New Paradigms," *Next*, November-December 1998, p. 4. (Originally Published in *Forbes*, October 5, 1998.)
[2] John N. Vaughan, *Megachurches and America's Cities* (Grand Rapids MI: Baker Books, 1993), p. 15.
[3] Ted Haggard, "New Year's Resolutions for a New Millennium," *Charisma,* December 1999, p. 60.
[4] Lyle E. Schaller, *The Multiple Staff and the Larger Church* (Nashville TN: Abingdon Press, 1980), p. 28
[5] Gary L. McIntosh, *One Size Doesn't Fit All* (Grand Rapids MI: Fleming H. Revell, 1999), p.65.

CHAPTER FIVE

AN APOSTOLIC VISION FOR CITY TRANSFORMATION

If we have come to terms with the three crucial concepts, apostles of the city, territorial commitment, and extra-denominational affiliations, we are ready to visualize what a city transformation process might look like in a new wineskin. "Where there is no vision, the people perish" (Pr. 29:18, KJV). I mention this because I do not have a clear successful case study to report as yet. I have faith that there will be many of them sooner than we think. So, I admit that, for now, this is just my own personal vision of how this could work and work well. But if we don't visualize it, it will never happen!

What, then, might an apostolic city transformation initiative look like?

1. The Apostles of the City Are in Place

Apostles are a gift from God, specifically from the risen Christ, to the church. "[Jesus ascended on high] and He Himself gave some to be apostles, some prophets, some evangelists, and some pastors and teachers" (Eph. 4:11). From this I would conclude that the apostles of the church in the city are given by God, and if that is the case, His people there should recognize them as such.

Here is what it would look like if the apostles of the city were in place:

♦ The apostles of the city would recognize themselves as apostles. I will be the first to admit that this is not always easy. I tell the story of my own journey toward recognizing that I was an apostle in my book, *Apostles and Prophets: The Foundation of the Church* (Regal Books), a journey that took about six years. Quite a few might say, "I have apostolic ministry," but they would stop short of saying, "I am an apostle." When I wrote my book, *The New Apostolic Churches* (Regal Books), I asked eighteen apostles to contribute chapters. At that time, only two of the eighteen would let me use the title "apostle" with their name. This, however, is changing quite rapidly.

♦ Other apostles would recognize them as apostles. I have said that I believe that in a sizeable city there will ordinarily be more than one apostle of the city. Not only is it important that they themselves know they are apostles, but it is equally important that they affirm, support, and encourage each other. If they understand apostolic spheres, as they should, there will not be a sense of competition among them, but rather a sense of camaraderie.

♦ A significant number of pastors and other Christian leaders in the city recognize them as apostles of the city. This is absolutely necessary. The proof that anyone is an apostle is that there are those who are committed to follow the apostle's leadership. No followers, no apostle! I do not know what percentage of the church leaders of a city need to be actively involved in this, but in any case, it needs to be enough to produce a critical mass, but not necessarily 100 percent.

♦   Their spheres are defined and mutually recognized. Apostles function best when things are in order. Each apostle recognizing and being able to clearly define their sphere of activity is a prerequisite for success. For example, I live in Colorado Springs, and, although I am not involved in the city per se, I can easily recognize at least four apostolic spheres in the city. I would suspect that further investigation would show that there are more. One is The Net and a second is the Colorado Springs Association of Evangelicals which are so closely related that some might consider them as one. A third is the El Paso County Ministerial Fellowship to which many of the African-American pastors belong. Another embraces the old first churches of downtown in which pastors with a more liberal theological bent relate to each other. A similar picture would emerge in almost any American city.

2. The Apostles Find a Way to Minister as Apostles

In the early chapters I tried to make it as clear as I could that a major reason why apostles of the city often keep an arm's length distance from those who are managing the city transformation initiative in their city is because if they were in it, they would not be allowed to provide apostolic leadership. They would simply be a cog in a machine that tries to please everyone who joins, to keep peace, and to discover a least common denominator with which everyone can agree. When invited to something like this, most apostles will say "Thanks, but no thanks." The apostles I know would rather do almost anything else other than serve as a member of someone else's committee.

My vision for this is that we cease trying to organize one, central coordinating committee to implement the city taking process. Rather, we would mutually encourage the spontaneous formation of apostolic units, each of which would be a group of like-minded pastors led by an apostle of the city. This is a very promising way of doing what we know that we need to do, namely organizing the spiritual gatekeepers of the city for action. But it goes without saying that this cannot happen unless and until apostles of the city are recognized and affirmed.

If this works well, here is what would be happening in each apostolic unit or sphere:

- ◆ The apostle would be mentoring the pastors. Many pastors would welcome this, especially if it would provide an opportunity for small church pastors to have regular, constructive contact with a megachurch pastor whom they admire. Under present conditions in most cities, this never happens.

- ◆ The apostle holds the pastors accountable. It is true that many of the pastors would be under an accountability system in their own denomination, but given the nature of the new extra-denominational affiliations, this kind of relationship might turn out to be even more meaningful and effective for them. The pastors in a given apostolic unit would also build an accountability to each other.

- ◆ The apostles make themselves personally available to

the pastors in their sphere. The litmus test of whether they really are available is whether they return phone calls. Some apostles need considerable improvement in this area.

♦ The apostles identify personally with the successes and failures of the pastors in their unit. This comes naturally to a true apostle. The greatest joy to an apostle is to add value to the life and ministry of a follower.

♦ The members of each unit feel comfortable with each other every time they meet. The meeting is a personal highlight for all who participate. It gets top priority for scheduling. In this system, no one has to check any distinctives at the door.

The Size

If these apostolic units begin to form in the city, what should their size be? According to group dynamics theory, each unit should run from a low of 10-15 to a high of 30-40. The low numbers represent the critical mass for a meaningful, ongoing group. The high numbers represent the maximum group size for sustaining meaningful personal relationships. Above that, the group transitions from a primary group to a secondary group and in a secondary group many members do not even know each other's names.

These numbers begin to give us a handle on how many apostolic units our city might expect. Let's say a city has 300 churches, and half of them want to be a part of the city transformation process. It would be reasonable, in that case, to look for 5-10 apostolic units in operation.

A major reason why this structure has such a high potential for success is that each one of the apostolic units is cohesive enough to act quickly and decisively whenever their apostle gives the word for action.

Let me point out that, as this model develops, unity is no longer an end in itself. There is no pressure to get all the pastors of a city together with all others. The Billy Graham committee ceases to be the ideal. Functioning apostolic units become the building blocks for the future rather than a central committee.

3. The Apostles Develop a City Apostolic Council

Admittedly, we are moving into uncharted waters at this point. But my vision sees the apostles who lead the several apostolic units in the city coming together with each other on a strictly peer-level basis. It would most likely take a gifted horizontal apostle to bring together the city's vertical apostles. The horizontal apostle would not control the group or even lead it, but rather moderate it.

What this would produce would be a small group of peer-level visionary, initiating, risk-taking, task-oriented leaders. They would not threaten each other because they are secure and they have nothing to prove.

It is worth mentioning that up to this point, political correctness would not be a major issue. But when we get to this level, it kicks in. The city apostolic council, if city transformation is to occur, would need to represent all the principal population segments of the city if it is to reach its maximum potential.

A group of apostles like this would need no outside help in designing a functional plan for city transformation. The most creative city leadership is in place. They are pragmatic through and through. They know how to get a job done.

♦ They will appoint the right administrators. Very few apostles are administrators, but they know how to get others to do their administrative work.

♦ They will provide the necessary finances. Money is no problem to the typical apostle. Fund-raising is usually an uphill battle without apostles involved. With them, the money is there and there quickly.

♦ They will invite appropriate outside resources at the appropriate times in the city transformation process. This will be a big change from the largely directionless and uncoordinated contributions from outside parachurch ministries that we have been seeing in our cities across the country. If the apostles give the word for a training event or a celebration, the presence and participation of the pastors of the city will not be a question.

♦ The apostles will enjoy this greatly, because apostles enjoy doing what they do best. They are leading, they are wheeling and dealing, they can make decisions without committees, they catalyze action, and they see tangible results.

When all of this happens, the city will then have the proper leadership in place for revival and city transformation.

Conclusion:
The Bottom Line Question

After reading this, many will be asking the question, "Is my city prepared for the moving of the Holy Spirit that will bring authentic city transformation in the near future?" The answer to this is another, bottom-line question:

Is the territorial, city wide apostolic leadership recognized, functioning, and coordinated in our city?

If the answer is "yes," transformation can soon come. If the answer is "no," my advice is to get busy and change what needs to be changed in order to allow God to step in and to make your city everything He wants it to be!

Wagner Publications Presents:

RIDDING YOUR HOME OF SPIRITUAL DARKNESS
Chuck D. Pierce
& Rebecca Wagner Sytsema

Christians are often completely unaware of how the enemy has gained access to their homes through what they own. This practical, easy-to-read book can be used by any Christian to pray through their home and property in order to close the door to the enemy and experience richer spiritual life. Included are chapters on children, sin, generational curses, and spiritual discernment, as well as a step-by-step guide to praying through your home.

Paperback (75 pp.) • 0.9667481.7.4 • $7.00

RECEIVING THE WORD OF THE LORD
Chuck D. Pierce
& Rebecca Wagner Sytsema

The Bible makes it very clear that God has a plan for our lives. By hearing and receiving the voice of God, we can know our purpose and destiny. In this book you will discover how to hear the voice of God, develop an understanding of prophecy, learn how to test a prophetic word, and experience the joy of responding to God's voice.

Paperback (41 pp.) • 0.9667481.2.3 • $6.00

From C. Peter Wagner . . .

RADICAL HOLINESS FOR RADICAL LIVING
C. Peter Wagner

Can anyone really live a holy life? Is there a test of holiness? *Radical Holiness for Radical Living* answers these and other questions as it opens the way for you to move to new levels in your Christian life. You can defeat Satan's schemes and enjoy daily victory in your walk with God.
Paperback (41 pp.) · 0.9667481.1.5 · $6.00

HARD-CORE IDOLATRY: FACING THE FACTS
C. Peter Wagner

This hard-hitting book is destined to clear away the foggy thinking about idolatry that has permeated churches today. This book will help you recognize idolatry (even in some of our churches), confront the schemes of the enemy with more understanding and power, feel the pain of God's broken heart when His people worship idols, and begin to cleanse your home of idolatrous objects.
Paperback (43 pp.) · 0.9667481.4.X · $6.00

REVIVAL! IT CAN TRANSFORM YOUR CITY
C. Peter Wagner

This book answers many questions including: What exactly is revival? Can my city actually be transformed through revival? What steps can be taken to sustain revival in a city? Discover how the Spirit of God can visibly transform our cities through the revival for which we have been praying!
Paperback (63 pp.) · 0.9667481.8.2 · $6.00

Confronting the Queen of Heaven
C. Peter Wagner

This book takes a look at what is perhaps one of the most powerful spirits in Satan's hierarchy--the Queen of Heaven. This book answers what we as Christians can do to play a part in confronting the Queen of Heaven and proclaiming that Jesus Christ is Lord.
Paperback (42 pp.) • 0.9667481.3.1 • $6.00

A People of Destiny
Finding Your Place in God's Apostolic Order
Barbara Wentroble

This book reveals how God is empowering laypeople to minister His hope to a dying world as never before. Discover the characteristics of every-day believers who are making a real difference by using the unlimited possibilities available to today's Christian. Barbara Wentroble's insights shared in this book will help you become a person of destiny!
Paperback (57 pp.) · 1.58502.005.2 · $6.00

How to Cast Out Demons: A Beginner's Guide
Doris M. Wagner

Many modern Christians are now agreeing that we should take Jesus' command to cast out demons more seriously than we have. But how do we do it? Where do we start? This practical, down-to-earth book, written by a respected deliverance practitioner, will show you how.
Paperback (201 pp.) • 1.58502.002.8 • $12.00

HOW TO HAVE A DYNAMIC CHURCH PRAYER MINISTRY
Jill Griffith

The local church has a unique opportunity to foster prayer that can dramatically move the heart of God. This book offers creative and proven step-by-step guidelines to help you mobilize and train effective intercessors, launch and maintain a thriving prayer room, and make a difference both inside and outside the church walls.
Paperback (66 pp.) • 0.9667481.9.0 • $6.00

THE AUTHORITY OF THE BELIEVER AND HEALING
Che Ahn

We live in an uprecedented hour for healing and miracles when God is lavishly distributing His gifts upon believers everywhere. Find out how you can play a part in this move of God, and how you can access your inheritance in the power of the Spirit through this insightful teaching.
Paperback (55 pp.) • 1.58502.003.6 • $6.00

Other titles available from Wagner Publications: